# THE SPREAD OF
# COVID-19

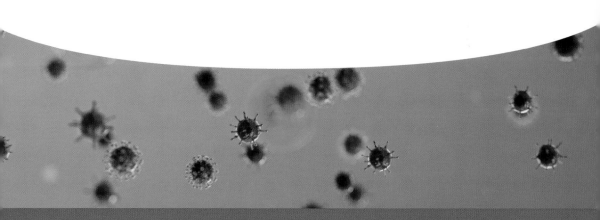

**BY MARTHA LONDON**

**CONTENT CONSULTANT**
Mark N. Lurie, PhD
Associate Professor of Epidemiology, International Health Institute
Brown University School of Public Health

Cover image: A temporary hospital in Iran was set up in preparation for COVID-19 patients.

Core Library

An Imprint of Abdo Publishing
abdobooks.com

abdobooks.com

Published by Abdo Publishing, a division of ABDO, PO Box 398166, Minneapolis, Minnesota 55439. Copyright © 2021 by Abdo Consulting Group, Inc. International copyrights reserved in all countries. No part of this book may be reproduced in any form without written permission from the publisher. Core Library™ is a trademark and logo of Abdo Publishing.

Printed in the United States of America, North Mankato, Minnesota
072020
092020

THIS BOOK CONTAINS
RECYCLED MATERIALS

Cover Photo: Ebrahim Noroozi/AP Images
Interior Photos: Shi Zhi/Feature China/AP Images, 4–5; iStockphoto, 7, 14–15; Ricardo Castelan Cruz/Eyepix/Cover Images/Newscom, 9; 770 Productions/Newscom, 10; Red Line Editorial, 12, 35; Hector Retamal/AFP/Getty Images, 17; Gemunu Amarasinghe/AP Images, 18; Koki Kataoka/The Yomiuri Shimbun/AP Images, 20, 45; Ben Powell/Odessa American/AP Images, 22–23, 43; Nicolò Campo/Sipa USA/AP Images, 25; Rick Bowmer/AP Images, 26; Alex Brandon/AP Images, 30–31; John Lamparski/NurPhoto/AP Images, 33; Ted S. Warren/AP Images, 36, 40; Bill Oxford/iStockphoto, 38

Editor: Angela Lim
Series Designer: Jake Nordby

Library of Congress Control Number: 2020936521

Publisher's Cataloging-in-Publication Data

Names: London, Martha, author.
Title: The spread of COVID-19 / by Martha London
Description: Minneapolis, Minnesota : Abdo Publishing, 2021 | Series: Core Library Guide to COVID-19 | Includes online resources and index
Identifiers: ISBN 9781532194061 (lib. bdg.) | ISBN 9781644945032 (pbk.) | ISBN 9781098212971 (ebook)
Subjects: LCSH: Disease (Pathology)—Juvenile literature. | Medical personnel--Juvenile literature. | Public health--Juvenile literature. | Biomedical research--Juvenile literature. | Communicable diseases--Prevention--Juvenile literature. | Epidemics--Juvenile literature. | COVID-19 (Disease)--Juvenile literature.
Classification: DDC 614.44--dc23

# CONTENTS

# MORE CASES, NOT ENOUGH BEDS

Bulldozers droned through the night in January 2020. Workers cleared a huge space of land. They were building a new hospital in Wuhan, China. The city was the center of a virus outbreak.

In late 2019 and early 2020, hundreds of people in Wuhan became sick. Some of them died. Doctors discovered that a new virus was causing respiratory illnesses. Respiratory diseases affect a person's lungs and airways. They make people cough. Some patients have

Construction workers took just ten days to build a hospital for COVID-19 patients in Wuhan, China.

trouble breathing. Health officials named the new virus SARS-CoV-2. They called the illness it caused COVID-19.

Officials in Wuhan had trouble containing the outbreak. The hospitals in Wuhan were filled. Doctors needed more beds to care for patients. The new hospital would be for only COVID-19 patients.

The builders worked through the night. They finished the hospital in just ten days. The new hospital had 1,000 beds

# PERSPECTIVES

## NEW INFORMATION

The director of the Wuhan Central Hospital, Dr. Ai Fen, worked closely with others studying the outbreak. They wanted to understand the new coronavirus. Ai was one of the first to recognize how dangerous the virus was. Early on, doctors believed the virus was only transmitted by animals. In an interview, she said, "We watched more and more patients come in as the radius of the spread of infection became larger. . . . I knew there must be human to human transmission."

Many people who became sick with COVID-19 had mild symptoms, such as a cough.

available for patients. Those beds would soon be very important.

## WHAT IS COVID-19?

The name COVID-19 stands for "coronavirus disease 2019." The virus that causes COVID-19 belongs to a group of viruses called coronaviruses. The virus was discovered in December 2019.

Most patients with COVID-19 have mild symptoms. They may develop a cough and fever. These people recover with rest. Some people do not feel sick at all. But they still carry the disease. These people can pass the virus to others without knowing.

Approximately 20 percent of COVID-19 patients develop severe or critical symptoms. They may have a high fever. They might develop pneumonia. Pneumonia happens when fluid enters a person's lungs. People with COVID-19 may struggle to breathe. In these cases, they must go to a hospital for care.

## WHAT'S IN A NAME?

Coronaviruses are a group of viruses. They cause many different illnesses. Many affect the respiratory system. *Corona* is Latin for "crown." Coronaviruses have a unique appearance. These viruses have many rods sticking out from their main structures. Under a microscope, the virus looks like a crown.

## HOW DOES COVID-19 SPREAD?

Scientists discovered that COVID-19 came from animals. People get diseases from animals in several ways. They could touch or eat an infected animal. Or they could touch

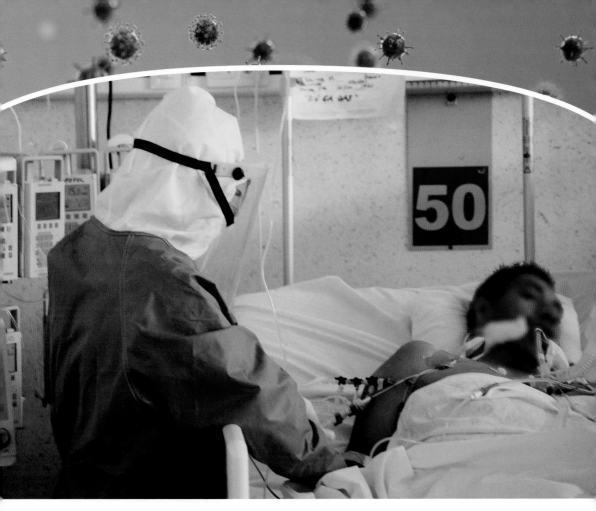

People with severe symptoms of COVID-19 have trouble breathing. They have to be treated in hospitals.

surfaces or foods that an infected animal has licked or pooped on. This contact can give people the virus.

Scientists believe the virus came from bats. Bat droppings or spit could have landed on fruits and vegetables. Bats could have infected other animals that were sold as food. People who ate those foods became

sick with COVID-19. Officials worked to stop the spread from animals. They closed markets that sold live animals. But the virus continued to infect more people.

Further research showed that the virus could also be spread from person to person. The virus is spread through coughs and sneezes. Tiny droplets land on surfaces. The virus can get on people's hands if they touch these surfaces. If people then touch their eyes, nose, or mouth, they can become ill. The viruses that cause the flu and common cold are also spread in this way. However, SARS-CoV-2 spreads more easily than those other viruses. People with the flu usually spread the disease when they are showing symptoms. But COVID-19 symptoms do not appear right away. People can infect others before knowing they are sick.

As the virus began to spread around the world, health officials told people how to stay healthy. People should wash their hands frequently. They should

Face masks and gloves offered protection against the virus. They prevented droplets of the virus from spreading to others.

# A RAPID RISE

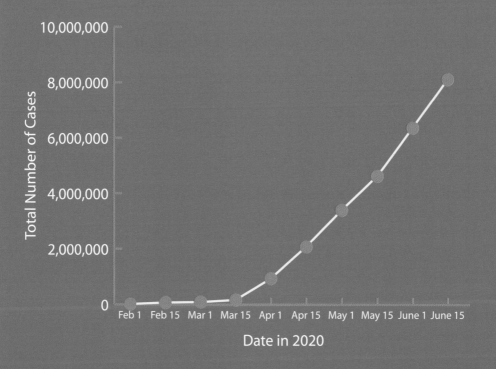

SARS-CoV-2 spread around the world quickly. By mid-June 2020, more than 8 million people had been infected with the virus. The graph above shows the number of total COVID-19 cases over time. What do you notice about the graph? How does the image help you better understand the main text?

wash for at least 20 seconds. They should avoid large gatherings of people. This lowers the amount of people who might come in contact with the virus. Officials told people to practice social distancing. Social distancing means staying at least 6 feet (1.8 m) away from others.

It is also called physical distancing. People were asked to only make necessary trips. They were also told to wear face masks in public. This blocks droplets from leaving the mouth and nose.

COVID-19 spreads quickly. Within a few months, millions of people around the world were affected by the disease. Scientists continued to study the disease and the virus that causes it in order to slow the spread.

## EXPLORE ONLINE

Chapter One discusses how COVID-19 is transmitted from person to person. The website below describes COVID-19 in more detail. What information does the website give about COVID-19? How is the information from the website the same as the information in Chapter One? What new information did you learn from the website?

## JUST FOR KIDS: A COMIC EXPLORING THE NEW CORONAVIRUS

abdocorelibrary.com/spread-of-covid-19

# TRYING TO CONTAIN THE VIRUS

In December 2019, only a few patients in China were sick. They had pneumonia and other respiratory symptoms. The patients seemed to mainly live in the city of Wuhan.

Chinese doctors did not recognize the new virus. The doctors contacted Chinese government officials. Health officials in the government needed to be prepared for the new virus.

Wuhan is one of the largest cities in China. It has a population of approximately 11 million people.

# SEARCHING FOR A SOURCE

At first the Chinese government did little to contain the disease. Infections ballooned by the end of December. Hospitals were filling up. Chinese officials reported the new disease to the World Health Organization (WHO) on December 31. The WHO works to help countries around the world fight diseases.

By early January 2020, hundreds of people were infected.

The Wuhan market linked to COVID-19 sold live fish and other seafood.

Doctors in China discovered it was a new coronavirus. It was similar to a virus that caused severe acute respiratory syndrome (SARS). SARS had spread around the world from 2002 to 2004. Hundreds of people died from the disease. But the WHO was eventually able to stop the spread.

Chinese officials linked many of the first COVID-19 patients to a Wuhan market. Several patients had gone

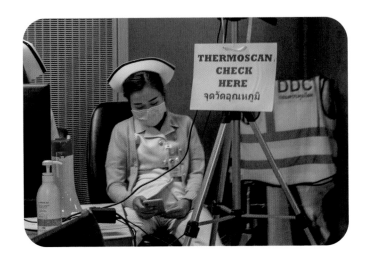

Officials in Thailand began checking the temperatures of travelers from China. People who were ill would be quarantined.

there before getting sick. So officials closed the market. They hoped this would stop the spread. But doctors continued to diagnose new cases.

## BEYOND BORDERS

International travel allowed the virus to spread around the world. People visiting Wuhan returned to their home countries. Some travelers did not know they were infected. In mid-January 2020, Japan and Thailand reported their first COVID-19 cases. These were the first known cases outside of China. Health officials in those countries began checking everybody flying in from

# TRACKING A PANDEMIC

I n early February, health officials in other countries confirmed cases of COVID-19. South Korea, Iran, and Italy reported their first deaths from the disease. Many countries took action to contain the spread. Some had more success than others.

## LOCKDOWN IN ITALY

By March 9, 2020, Italy had the second-highest number of COVID-19 cases. More than 400 people had died. Italy's prime minister

Cities around the world purchased masks and protective equipment for residents and health-care workers.

## ISOLATION, QUARANTINE, AND SHELTER IN PLACE

The words *isolation*, *quarantine*, and *shelter in place* have similar definitions. But they are used differently. All of these terms mean to stay inside. *Isolation* applies to a person with COVID-19 symptoms. He or she stays away from others to avoid spreading the disease. *Quarantine* applies to travelers and people who may have had contact with a sick person. Symptoms may appear up to 14 days after contact. After 14 days, the person knows he or she is not infected with the disease. *Shelter in place* applies to everyone. It means to stay inside except for doctor appointments or groceries.

made a controversial decision. He ordered the entire country to shelter in place. People who shelter in place can only leave their homes for things such as groceries or doctor appointments. Some local officials had already enforced shelter-in-place rules. But now, all of Italy's 60 million citizens could only leave their homes for essentials.

Large gatherings were postponed. Weddings and funerals were rescheduled.

Italian residents passed time together on their balconies while sheltering in place.

Tourism came to a halt. Some reporters wrote that the lockdown was one of the most severe measures taken in Italy since World War II (1939–1945).

Italian officials extended the lockdown through April. Police enforced the lockdown. People who went against the orders were ticketed.

Airports were almost completely empty during the pandemic. Many countries restricted travel.

Then the WHO made an announcement. It declared that COVID-19 was a pandemic on March 11, 2020. Nearly every country had reported at least one case of COVID-19. The disease was a worldwide emergency.

Spain's prime minister declared a state of emergency on March 14. Two weeks later, the prime minister ordered people to stay inside. Businesses closed. Travel was limited. Only essential workers could leave their homes. But the disease continued to spread. COVID-19 seemed to be out of control.

# A HALT ON GLOBAL TRAVEL

Many nations limited travel to slow the spread of the disease. Officials told citizens not to leave the country unless it was necessary. Special rules were made for US citizens returning from overseas. Some travelers would have to quarantine themselves. Officials wanted to make sure travelers did not spread the virus when they returned home.

Thousands of flights were canceled. Cruise ship companies were also affected. On March 13, 2020,

## PERSPECTIVES

### A CRUISE SHIP OUTBREAK

In February 2020, the *Diamond Princess* cruise ship was ready to dock in Japan. But doctors reported cases of COVID-19 on board the ship. All 3,711 passengers and crew members were ordered to stay on board. After more than two weeks, a total of 712 passengers tested positive for the coronavirus. Disease researcher Dr. Amesh Adalja said that staying on board the ship made the outbreak worse. He said, "The quarantine . . . allow[ed] the virus to literally pick [the passengers] off one-by-one."

a major cruise organization stopped cruise travel for 30 days. Other cruise companies postponed cruises for longer periods of time.

Countries reduced personal travel. But the WHO suggested that global trade continue. Limiting overseas trade could prevent countries from receiving health equipment. Many countries faced shortages of masks and other medical supplies.

## SLOWING THE SPREAD

At the beginning of April, Europe had the highest death toll of any continent. Approximately 60 percent of COVID-19 deaths came from European countries. But Europeans were hopeful that the spread of COVID-19 would slow.

At the end of the first week of April, Spain reported its lowest number of new cases and deaths since its lockdown. The strict measures had slowed the spread of the virus. But there was a long way to go before countries would be rid of the virus.

# STRAIGHT TO THE
# SOURCE

On March 11, 2020, the WHO labeled COVID-19 a pandemic. WHO director-general Tedros Adhanom Ghebreyesus explained in a speech the reasoning for the label. He said:

> WHO has been assessing this outbreak around the clock and we are deeply concerned both by the alarming levels of spread and severity, and by the alarming levels of inaction. We have therefore made the assessment that COVID-19 can be characterized as a pandemic. . . . Describing the situation as a pandemic does not change WHO's assessment of the threat posed by this virus. It doesn't change what WHO is doing, and it doesn't change what countries should do.

Source: Tedros Adhanom Ghebreyesus. "WHO Director-General's Opening Remarks at the Media Briefing on COVID-19 — 11 March 2020." *World Health Organization*, 11 Mar. 2020, who.int. Accessed 8 Apr. 2020.

## BACK IT UP

The speaker of this passage is using evidence to support a point. Write a paragraph describing the point being made. Then write down two or three pieces of evidence used to make the point.

3/2

3/3

3/4

3/5

3/6

PRESIDENT OF THE UNITE

# A NEW EPICENTER

**T**he number of COVID-19 cases in the United States grew throughout March. By March 26, the United States had the most cases of any country. The United States became the new epicenter of the pandemic.

## SPREADING THROUGH THE UNITED STATES

The first US case of COVID-19 was confirmed in January 2020. The earliest US patients had traveled to Wuhan. But by late February,

Dr. Anthony Fauci, the director of the National Institute of Allergy and Infectious Diseases, discussed the COVID-19 outbreak during a presentation on March 31, 2020.

31

California confirmed its first case from a person who had not traveled outside the country. This meant the virus was spreading from person to person in the United States.

At first most US cases were in Washington and California. As a result, the governor of California issued a statewide shelter-in-place order on March 19. The governor of Washington issued a shelter-in-place order for his state shortly afterward on March 23.

Cities with large populations were most affected. People in cities live close together. Many take public transportation, where it is difficult to maintain social distancing. A person may interact with many people in a single day. Those without symptoms could accidentally spread the disease to many others.

On March 1, 2020, New York officials confirmed the state's first coronavirus case. The number of cases

In early April, New York City had approximately 50 percent of the state's COVID-19 cases. Many people had to be taken to the hospital for treatment.

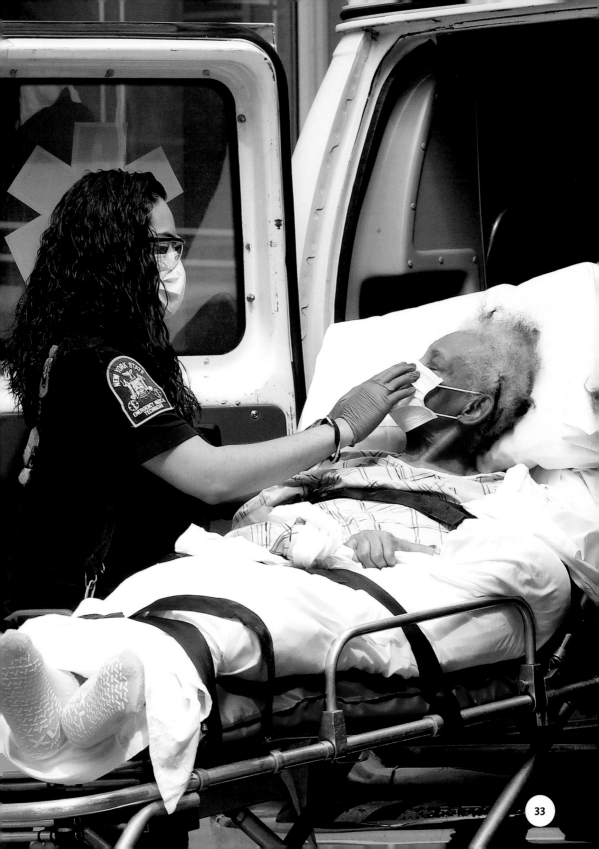

quickly jumped to 1,000 and continued increasing. New York officials canceled the Saint Patrick's Day Parade.

The Statue of Liberty was closed to visitors. The governor ordered citizens to stay home. By mid-March, all 50 US states had reported at least one COVID-19 case. Individual states created their own responses to slow the spread. The federal government did not issue a stay-at-home recommendation.

# CASES BY COUNTRY THROUGH JUNE 30, 2020

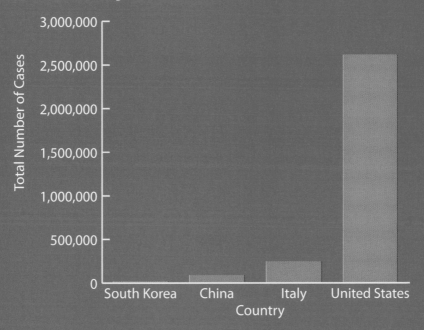

The graph above shows the number of confirmed cases in certain countries through June 30, 2020. The initial outbreak was in China. How does the number of COVID-19 cases in China compare to other countries? After reading this book, how does this graph help you better understand the information in the text?

## LACK OF TESTING

Some countries tested hundreds of thousands of

people at the beginning of the outbreak. This let health

officials know who had the disease and how quickly it

was spreading. People who tested positive were placed

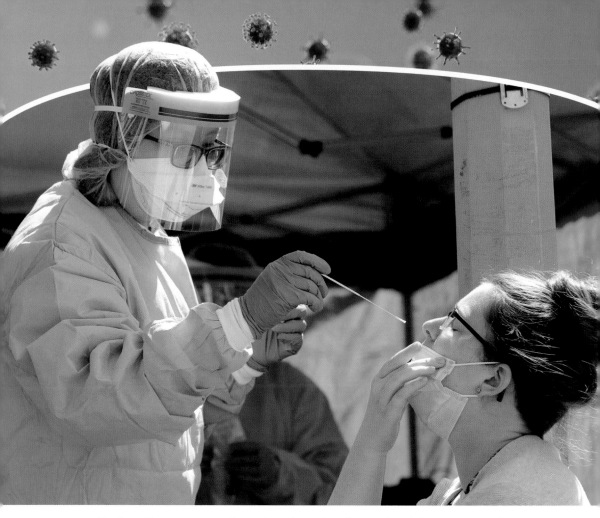

Early efforts to combat the virus in the United States were hurt by shortages of testing supplies.

in isolation. Officials also tried to locate people who interacted with a patient. Those people could be tested and quarantined. Broad testing allowed countries to effectively slow the spread of COVID-19.

The Centers for Disease Control and Prevention (CDC) worked to make widespread testing possible in the United States. However, the first test kits didn't work properly. US states had difficulty accessing tests. States turned to private companies for tests. The CDC worked to develop new test kits. But supplies remained limited. The lack of testing allowed the virus to spread quickly in the United States.

Tests were often only given to people with symptoms. But many people with COVID-19 did not show symptoms for several days. Some did not show symptoms

## POSTPONING THE OLYMPICS

On March 24, 2020, the International Olympic Committee (IOC) and Japanese officials postponed the 2020 Olympics. They were originally set to begin in July 2020. The IOC hoped to hold the games in 2021. At the time of the decision, COVID-19 had spread to every continent except Antarctica. Nearly 20,000 people had died. Almost 400,000 people had been infected. Major sports leagues around the world canceled or postponed their seasons.

LOT: CT788549
SARS-CoV-2
CLINICAL
TRIALS
COVID-19

TEST: 9-18-2020
PATIENT # SS87-23

LOT: CT788549
SARS-CoV-2
CLINICAL
TRIALS
COVID-19

TEST: 7-18-2020
PATIENT # SS87-23

at all. They could still spread the disease. Testing those without symptoms is necessary to stop the spread.

## WHAT HAPPENS NEXT?

Death and infection rates declined in some European and Asian countries in April 2020. Meanwhile infection rates in South America increased. Some countries slowly allowed people to return to work. Travel was still limited. Social distancing continued. Officials asked people to be patient.

Health officials warned there could be a second outbreak. Countries could resume activities too soon. The virus could come back. Many more people could die.

Organizations around the world did not want another outbreak of COVID-19. Vaccine research began in late February 2020. Scientists worked to create a vaccine as quickly as possible.

Companies around the world worked to create a vaccine against COVID-19.

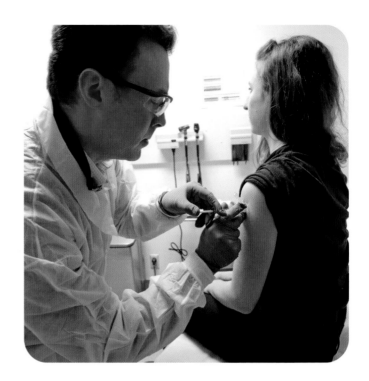

A doctor in Washington State administers a trial vaccine for COVID-19.

But it takes an average of four years to develop a vaccine. Medical experts hoped that global efforts to make a vaccine would speed up the process. But they still said it was unlikely a vaccine would be available within the first year of research. The United Kingdom began vaccine trials at the end of April. Scientists planned to continue researching vaccines and potential drug treatments. They wanted to slow the spread of COVID-19. Scientists wanted the world to be safe from the coronavirus.

# STRAIGHT TO THE
# SOURCE

In March 2020, Jennifer Haller became the first person to receive a test vaccine for COVID-19. In an interview, Haller talked about her choice to be a vaccine trial participant:

> Some friends were definitely concerned. I explained that the vaccine uses messenger RNA, which means throughout the whole trial I'll never be exposed to the actual virus. . . . And yes—this has never been tested on humans, so there's a complete unknown.
>
> But you know, my understanding is that it's similar to what they've done with MERS and SARS, and that the good that can come from it is so much greater than anything that can happen to me. . . . I'm not doing it in the hopes of protecting myself, I'm not expecting that. Right now, they're just trying to figure out what dosage they need to give for it to be effective.

Source: Mirel Zaman. "I Was the First Person to Test the Coronavirus Vaccine." *Refinery 29*, 17 Mar. 2020, refinery29.com. Accessed 9 Apr. 2020.

## WHAT'S THE BIG IDEA?

Read the text carefully. What's the main idea? Explain how Haller supports the main idea with details. Write a short paragraph naming two or three of those supporting details.

# FAST FACTS

- COVID-19 is the disease caused by a newly discovered coronavirus called SARS-CoV-2.

- The first confirmed case of COVID-19 was identified in Wuhan, China, in December 2019.

- The first cases outside of China appeared in Thailand and Japan.

- On March 11, 2020, the WHO declared COVID-19 a pandemic.

- Countries across the world instituted shelter-in-place orders. Fewer people interacted. Countries hoped to contain the spread.

- Broad testing in countries such as South Korea helped slow the spread of the virus.

- COVID-19 cases were confirmed in the United States beginning in January 2020. Hundreds of thousands of people were infected in the next several months. The United States became the epicenter of the pandemic, reaching 1 million cases on April 29, 2020.

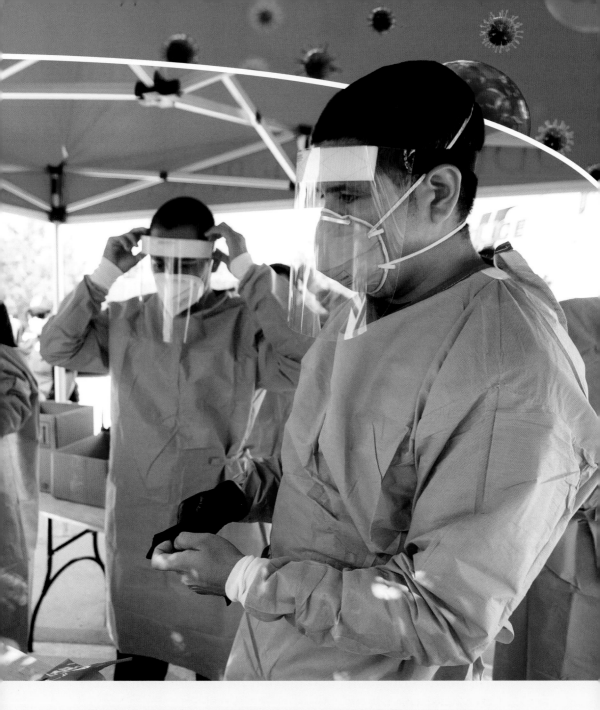

- By the end of June 2020, more than 10 million people had been diagnosed with COVID-19.

# STOP AND
# THINK

### Tell the Tale

Chapter One of this book discusses workers constructing an emergency hospital. Imagine you are one of the workers. Write 200 words about what it is like to be building a new hospital in only ten days.

### Take a Stand

Some people said leaders throughout the world acted too slowly to contain the virus. What do you think? Do you think leaders acted in time, or do you think more could have been done?

### Why Do I Care?

Maybe you do not know anyone who contracted COVID-19. But that doesn't mean you can't think about personal hygiene and staying healthy. How does washing your hands affect your life? Do you have friends or family members who have health conditions that make it harder for them to stay healthy? How might your life be different if you or a family member contracted COVID-19?

## You Are There

This book discusses how COVID-19 spread throughout the world. Imagine you and your friends are living in the middle of the pandemic. Write a letter to your friends talking about how COVID-19 has changed your life. What are some things that have stayed the same?

# GLOSSARY

**controversial**
causing opposing views

**emission**
gas released into the
atmosphere due to burning
fuels such as gasoline or coal

**epicenter**
the area that is most affected
by something

**pandemic**
a disease that spreads across
the world

**postpone**
to delay or reschedule
an event

**respiratory**
having to do with the lungs
and airways

**transmission**
how a virus is spread

# ONLINE RESOURCES

To learn more about the spread of COVID-19, visit our free resource websites below.

**Core Library**
CONNECTION
FREE! COMMON CORE MULTIMEDIA RESOURCES

Visit **abdocorelibrary.com** or scan this QR code for free Common Core resources for teachers and students, including vetted activities, multimedia, and booklinks, for deeper subject comprehension.

**Booklinks**
NONFICTION NETWORK
FREE! ONLINE NONFICTION RESOURCES

Visit **abdobooklinks.com** or scan this QR code for free additional online weblinks for further learning. These links are routinely monitored and updated to provide the most current information available.

# LEARN MORE

Bennett, Howard. *The Fantastic Body*. Rodale, 2017.

*Human Body!* DK Children, 2017.

London, Martha. *Flattening the Curve*. Abdo Publishing, 2021.

# INDEX

## About the Author

Martha London is a writer and educator. She lives in Minnesota with her cat.